FOOTBALL:
THE BEAUTIFUL GAME

What's the most exciting word in the English language? If your answer is 'Goal!', then you're already a fan of the beautiful game.

And you are not alone. There are millions of people like you all over the world – playing football, watching it, wearing the football shirts of their favourite team, travelling hundreds of kilometres to watch their club or their country play, or just kicking a football around on a beach or in the street.

So here is the story of the beautiful game – from its beginnings thousands of years ago to the international game of today. The rules, the players, the cups, the clubs, the stars, the fans – this is football, from Argentina to Zidane.

OXFORD BOOKWORMS LIBRARY
Factfiles

Football:
The Beautiful Game

Stage 2 (700 headwords)

Factfiles Series Editor: Christine Lindop

For Michael,
my favourite footballer

STEVE FLINDERS

Football:
The Beautiful Game

OXFORD UNIVERSITY PRESS

OXFORD
UNIVERSITY PRESS

Great Clarendon Street, Oxford OX2 6DP

Oxford University Press is a department of the University of Oxford.
It furthers the University's objective of excellence in research, scholarship,
and education by publishing worldwide in

Oxford New York

Auckland Cape Town Dar es Salaam Hong Kong Karachi
Kuala Lumpur Madrid Melbourne Mexico City Nairobi
New Delhi Shanghai Taipei Toronto

With offices in

Argentina Austria Brazil Chile Czech Republic France Greece
Guatemala Hungary Italy Japan Poland Portugal Singapore
South Korea Switzerland Thailand Turkey Ukraine Vietnam

OXFORD and OXFORD ENGLISH are registered trade marks of
Oxford University Press in the UK and in certain other countries

ISBN: 978 0 19 402294 1

A complete recording of this Bookworms edition of
Football: The Beautiful Game is available.

Printed in China

Word count (main text): 7,015

For more information on the Oxford Bookworms Library,
visit www.oup.com/elt/gradedreaders

ACKNOWLEDGEMENTS
Illustration p7 by Miguel Herranz/Storyboards.nl
The publishers would like to thank the following for permission to reproduce images:
akg-images p15; Corbis UK Ltd. pp9 (Roland Schlager/Epa), 10 (Rainer Jensen/Epa),
28 (Jean-Yves Ruszniewski/Tempsport), 29 (Michael Hanschke/Dpa),
30 (Catherine Ivill/Ama), 36 (Sebastiao Moreira/Epa);
Getty Images pp6 (Paula Bronstein/Reportage), 8 (Brendon Thorne),
13 (Laurence Griffiths), 14 (Popperfoto), 16 (Giuseppe Cacace/AFP),
18 (Alex Livesey), 19 (Khaled Desouki/AFP), 21 (Shaun Botterill),
22 (Bob Thomas/Popperfoto), 24 (Christof Koepsel/Bongarts), 25 (Paul Gilham),
31 (Vanderlei Almeida/AFP), 37 (Andrew Yates/AFP), 39 (Cesar Rangel/AFP),
40 (Sebastian Willnow/AFP); PA Photos ppviii (Mike Egerton),
3 (Guibbaud Christophe/ABACA), 4 (Walter G Arce/Landov),
26 (AP), 33; 34 (Kin Cheung/AP).

The manufacturer's authorised representative in the EU for product safety is
Oxford University Press España S.A. of el Parque Empresarial San Fernando de Henares,
Avenida de Castilla, 2 - 28830 Madrid (www.oup.es/en)

CONTENTS

1 The beautiful game

On 30 July 1930, 93,000 people went to the Estadio Centenario in Montevideo, Uruguay, to watch the final of the first FIFA World Cup. Uruguay beat Argentina 4–2, and was the first country to have its name on the World Cup.

There was no television then (the first World Cup on TV was not until 1954). There were forty-one countries in FIFA (from the French for International Federation of Association Football), the international organisation which controls football, but only thirteen countries played in the competition. The USA, Mexico, and seven South American countries sent teams to Uruguay, but only four teams came from Europe. Three of those teams – Belgium, France, and Romania – travelled across the Atlantic together in the same boat. The Brazilian team got on the boat in Rio de Janeiro.

The eighteenth World Cup final, seventy-six years later, was very different. On 9 July 2006, Italy played France in the Olympiastadion in Berlin, Germany. Italy beat France to win the World Cup for the fourth time. But the 2006 World Cup started with teams from 198 countries. At the finals in Germany there were fourteen teams from Europe, six from Africa and the Middle East, four from South America, four from North and Central America and the Caribbean, three from Asia, and one from Oceania (Australia). There were sixty-four matches in the competition, and 3.3 million tickets for the fans who came to watch. Fewer people – 74,000 – were in the stadium than for the final in 1930, because modern stadiums have to have seats for all the fans. But 400 million more watched the game on television. Perhaps eight out of ten people *in the world* watched part of a World Cup match this time.

Football is the world's favourite sport. There are more than 1.5 million football teams in the world and 300,000 football clubs – and then there are school teams and children's teams too. More than 240 million people play football in more than 200 countries, and more than 20 million of them are women. There are football teams for people who cannot see, and since 2003 there has been a Homeless World Cup for teams of people who have no homes. There are football newspapers and magazines, and radio and television stations just for football. There are millions and millions of football fans. Football is an international language.

Why do so many people love football? Because the rules are easy to understand and because the game is fast and exciting. It does not cost a lot to play – all you need is a ball and some players. Anyone can start a game of football, anywhere, any time. Football is not just about big teams and famous players. It is about small teams, about the fans, the stadiums, the cups, and the referees. For millions of people all over the world, football truly is 'the beautiful game'.

2 What kind of football?

Football, for most people, is association football or 'soccer'. A hundred years ago, some English university students took the 'soc' in association football and started calling this new game soccer. Soccer is one kind of football. In different parts of the world, people play other kinds of football.

In some countries, people play rugby football. The name comes from Rugby School in England, where it was first played around the 1840s. Rugby is played with a different ball; players can kick it, and they can also use their hands to pass it to another player. There are two kinds of rugby: rugby league, with thirteen players in a team, and rugby union, with fifteen players. For a long time, rugby union was an amateur game, and none of the

Scoring a try in rugby union

players got paid, but in the professional game of rugby league, clubs paid their players. In 1995 this changed, and now the top players in rugby union are professional too. In some countries rugby has more supporters than football. South Africa, Australia, and New Zealand always have strong rugby union teams and they play against one another every year in the Tri-Nations championship.

In the USA, a lot of people play and watch American football. In February each year 100 million people watch the Super Bowl, which is the final of the National Football League. American football is not played much outside the USA, but more and more people in other countries watch the Super Bowl. American football uses a ball like a rugby ball, and American footballers can kick the ball but also pass it with their hands. Teams are bigger too. It is a hard game and can be dangerous.

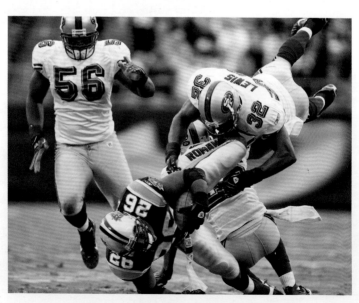

American football

In Ireland, people play Gaelic football. In this game, the ball is round and players can catch it but do not throw it. In Australia, there is a game called Australian rules football which has eighteen players in each team. Players can kick or hit the ball but not throw it. Australians like this kind of football best of all.

In this book, football means association football. Football is easy to understand, and there are only seventeen rules. It is played with a round ball on a football field or pitch. Each team has eleven players on the field. If a player is hurt and has to leave the field, another player – a substitute – can take his or her place. The team manager can also use a substitute if a player is tired or is not playing well. Usually a team can use three substitutes in a game.

A game lasts for 90 minutes: there are two halves of 45 minutes. If the referee stops the game because a player is hurt, they add more time – injury time – at the end of the 45 minutes. At half time the players have a rest for 15 minutes and when the game starts again, the teams change ends.

Each team tries to score goals, and at the end of the game the team with the most goals wins. If both teams get the same number of goals, or if neither team scores, the game is a draw. If there is a draw in a cup match after 90 minutes, the teams often go on playing for longer. This is called extra time. Sometimes they play for 30 minutes, and sometimes they stop when one team scores a goal: this is called a 'golden goal'.

You can play football in a team of eleven players on a football pitch with a referee. You can play with your friends in the street or on the beach. You can play five-a-side football or futsal. These games are shorter and the pitch is smaller so the games are very fast: the South Americans are very strong at five-a-side.

And if you don't feel like running around, you can play football games at home with your favourite teams and players. There is table football (Subbuteo); good Subbuteo players can play in a world championship every year. Or you can play your favourite computer football game, like Pro Evolution Soccer, which has sold over 12 million copies around the world.

3 Playing the game

Before the match starts, the two teams run onto the pitch. The referee controls the match, with two assistant referees to help. The referee blows a whistle to start the match.

If the ball goes outside the lines on the pitch, the assistant referee holds up their flag. When this happens, there is a throw-in. One player takes the ball in their hands and throws it back onto the field.

If the ball goes across the goal line, the rule is different. If a player from the attacking team touched the ball last, there is a goal kick. If a player from the defending team touched the ball last, there is a corner kick.

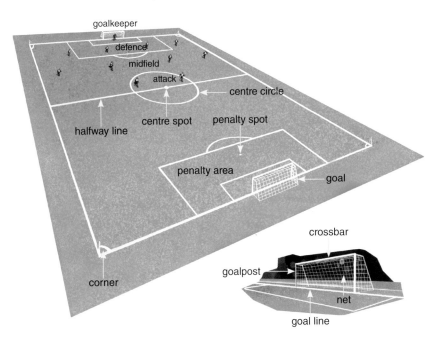

The assistant referee also holds up their flag if a player is offside. The offside rule is perhaps the most difficult rule in football. The rule says that when someone kicks the ball to an attacking player, there must be more than one player from the other team between the attacking player and the goal.

The referee blows the whistle to stop play when there is a foul. A foul is when a player does something wrong, for example when one player kicks another player, pushes them over, pulls their shirt, or touches the ball with their hands. When there is a foul, the referee gives a free kick to the other team. Sometimes a team can use a free kick to try to score a goal. If they are close to the goal, the other team will try to stop the ball with a 'wall' of players.

If the foul is in the penalty area (look at the picture of the football field on page 7), the referee gives a penalty to

A free kick

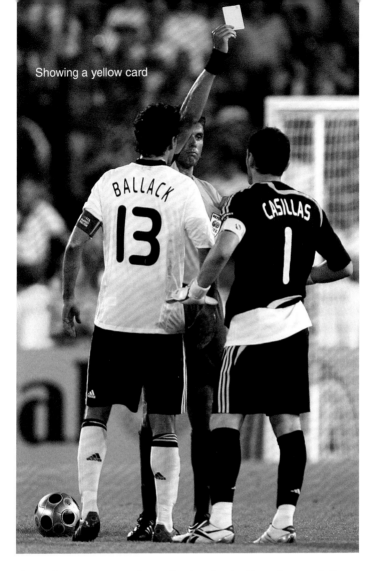

Showing a yellow card

the other team. A player kicks the ball at the goal from the penalty spot and only the goalkeeper can try and stop it. This is very difficult for the goalkeeper, so usually the team gets their goal.

If a player fouls another player badly, the referee shows them a yellow card. A player with two yellow cards has to leave the field. When a foul is very bad, the referee shows the player a red card and they have to leave the field at once.

Kinds of player

Football players can be big or small, tall or short, heavy or light. One of the good things about football is that small players can be just as good as big players. There are usually four kinds of player.

Each team has a goalkeeper. The goalkeeper is the only player who can take the ball in their hands on the football field. Their job is to stop the ball when the other team tries to score a goal. Goalkeepers are often tall, and they have to think and move very quickly. Some people say that you have to be a little bit crazy to be a good goalkeeper. The French-Algerian writer, Albert Camus, played in goal when he was young. He said later that playing football taught him many important lessons about life.

Goalkeeper, striker, and defender

Defenders play in front of the goalkeeper. They are often big and strong but they must also run fast. The defender's job is to stay close to the striker from the other team and get between them and their goal. If the defender does this well, the striker will find it difficult to score a goal.

Midfielders help both the defenders and the strikers. They are free to run up and down the field. They can make long passes like defenders or they can run with the ball like strikers. Team captains often play in midfield.

In the attack are the strikers. The job of the striker is to score goals. They try to get away from the defender who is close by, and they must be able to head the ball when it comes into the penalty area. Sometimes a striker has a very quiet game and does not do very much. Then suddenly the striker heads the ball or shoots, and the ball is in the net! A good striker knows how to be in the right place at the right time.

How teams play

Every team has defenders, a midfield and an attack, but the number of players in each part of the team is different. Between fifty and a hundred years ago, many teams played 2-3-5 with two defenders at the back, three in midfield and five at the front. In the 1950s, Hungary began to play 4-2-4 and Brazil won the 1958 World Cup playing like this, with two of the defenders sometimes in midfield to make a more attacking team. The England team that won the 1966 World Cup played 4-4-2, with more defenders and less attack. Today you can see 5-3-2, 4-4-2, 3-5-2 and others. Football is beautiful because every team is different!

4   The story of football

Football is very old. More than 2,000 years ago the Chinese were playing a ball game called *Tsu Chu* or *Cuju*. The Greeks, the Romans, and the Japanese also played ball games using their feet. In Britain by the year AD 217, village teams were playing football against other village teams. By the year 900 the Chinese were playing a kind of football game with rules, and with goalposts and nets.

By the 1300s, there was a lot of football in England and other European countries, but it was not the game that we know today. Sometimes there were hundreds of men in each team and there was a lot of fighting. Once a year in the town of Ashbourne in England they still play a game of football that is hundreds of years old. It takes two days, there are very few rules, and many players never see the ball!

The English kings did not like football, and many of them tried to stop the game. In 1314, the English king Edward the Third said that football was bad and dangerous. Too many people were getting hurt. Some years later, another English king, Richard the Second, said that all football must stop. But people did not listen. They went on playing football.

By the 1800s, there was a lot of football in schools in England but the rules were very different from one place to another. In some schools players could kick the ball

The Ashbourne football match

and throw it with their hands, but in others they could only kick it. So in October 1863 a group of men met in London to start the Football Association – the FA – and to write some rules for the game. They talked a lot about what players could and could not do, but after a number of meetings they said that association football players could not run with the ball in their hands. This was the beginning of modern football.

They quickly added new rules. An 1865 rule gave us the crossbar. The offside rule came in 1866, the goal kick in 1869, and the time of 90 minutes for a game in 1877.

In 1872, the FA decided to give a cup to the best team in England. Fifteen teams played against each other and the Wanderers won the first FA Cup Final (this team no longer exists). This is the oldest football cup competition in the world. It was also the year of the first international match – England against Scotland.

Notts County, FA Cup winners, 1894

At first all players were amateurs. Either they had other jobs and played in their free time, or they were already rich and did not need the money. But all kinds of men – rich and poor – now started to play football and by the 1880s, football clubs were paying men to play for them: these were the first professional footballers. In 1888, the English Football League began. It had twelve clubs: Accrington, Aston Villa, Blackburn Rovers, Bolton Wanderers, Burnley, Derby County, Everton, Notts County, Preston North End, Stoke City, West Bromwich Albion and Wolverhampton Wanderers. Eleven of these twelve teams (not Accrington) are still playing today. This was also the start of home games and away games for football teams. A home game is played in the team's own town; an away game is played in the other team's town. In 1891, the professional Blackburn Rovers beat the amateur Old Etonians in the FA Cup Final, the first time a professional team won the competition.

People began to play football in other countries. In 1865, a football club started in Buenos Aires. In 1872,

English sailors played football in Le Havre in France, and a football club began there. An English teacher in Montevideo started the first club in Uruguay in 1882. The Danish Football Association – the first in Europe – began in 1889. The game was moving across the world. Football became strong in France and in 1904, FIFA started in Paris. Today, FIFA's home is in Zurich in Switzerland. FIFA makes the rules of football for everyone.

Football was played at the Olympic Games for the first time in 1908. But only amateurs could play, so in 1930 there was the first world competition for professional footballers – the World Cup. From these small beginnings, football has got bigger and bigger. Today it is the number one international sport.

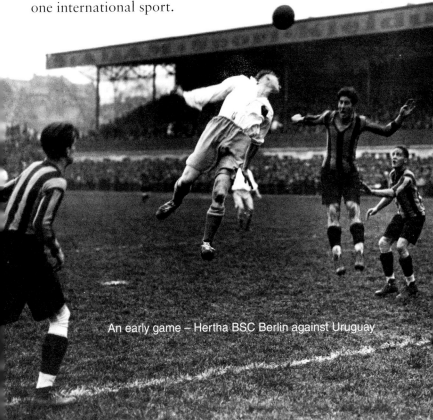

An early game – Hertha BSC Berlin against Uruguay

5   We won the cup

League competitions Most teams, amateur or professional, play in a league. The teams are usually in groups of about twenty. These groups are called divisions. Each team in a division plays every other team twice – once at home and once away. If there are twenty-two clubs in a division, then each team plays forty-two games during the football season. (In England the football season lasts from August to May, so the players can only rest in June and July.) Teams get three points when they win a game and one point when they draw. The team with the most points at the end of the season is the winner.

Inter and AC Milan in the Italian Serie A

In England, there are twenty professional clubs in the FA Premier League, which is the top division, and seventy-two more professional teams in the next three divisions of the Football League. Millions of people around the world watch the games of top clubs in the German Bundesliga and the Italian Serie A. But lots of fans also follow the games in leagues in their own countries, like the K-League in South Korea, the Egyptian Premier League, or the I-League in India.

Cup competitions

Most teams also play in one or two cup competitions during the football season. In a cup competition, there are a lot of teams at the beginning but only the winners of each game can play again. If there are thirty-two teams at the start, only sixteen teams play the next time. Then there are eight in the quarter-finals, four in the semi-finals, and two in the final.

The World Cup

The FIFA World Cup is the most famous cup competition in the world. The World Cup is every four years – 2002, 2006, 2010, etc. There have been eighteen World Cups since 1930 (there were no competitions between 1938 and 1950) and three countries – Brazil, Italy, and Germany – have played better than all the others. The greatest World Cup Final – and one of the great football matches of all time – was in 1970 between Brazil and Italy, when Brazil won 4–1. During the World Cup, the whole world goes crazy about football for a few weeks.

Brazil win the World Cup, 2002

But the top teams do not always win, and sometimes there are big surprises. North Korea beat Italy in 1966, Algeria beat West Germany in 1982, Cameroon beat Argentina in 1990 in the opening match, and in 1994 Bulgaria beat Germany in the quarter-finals.

Regional champions FIFA divides the world into six regions, and each region has a championship. In Europe, the UEFA European Football Championship is played every four years, two years after the World Cup. Germany has won this three times since it started in 1960, and France and Spain have won it twice.

The Copa América started in South America in 1916 and is the oldest international championship in the world. Uruguay and Argentina have both won this fourteen times. Until 2007, it was held every two years. Now it is every four years.

In Africa, the Africa Cup of Nations is played every two years. Egypt has won this six times since it started in 1957. The African Championship of Nations is also played every two years, but it is only for players who live and play in their home country.

In Asia, the Asian Cup has run since 1956. Saudi Arabia, Iran, and Japan have all won this competition three times, and South Korea has won twice.

Teams in North America play for the CONCACAF Gold Cup every two years, and both Mexico and the United States have won four times.

Finally, teams like New Zealand, Fiji, and Tahiti play for the OFC Nations Cup in the region of Oceania.

Club competitions
The oldest competition in the world is the FA Cup in England, but now there are international club competitions everywhere in the world.

The Africa Cup of Nations, Egypt, 2006

In Europe, the big club competitions are the UEFA Champions League (once called the European Cup) and the UEFA Cup. These are played every year. The Spanish team, Real Madrid, has won the Champions League/European Cup nine times since 1955.

In South America, the top clubs in the different countries play every year for the Copa Libertadores. The Argentinian club Independiente has won this seven times since 1960.

In Africa, the biggest competition is the CAF Champions League, which started in 1964. Two Egyptian clubs – Al Ahly and Al-Zamalek – have both won this competition five times.

In Asia, teams play for the AFC Cup and the AFC Champions League. Both competitions have changed a lot in recent years.

The FIFA Club World Cup is played every year between the winners of the big cup on each continent. This is a new competition and no team has won it more than once.

Olympic football
Football is also an Olympic sport. There has been football at every Olympics since 1908, but not in 1932. Professional players started to play at the Olympics in 1984 in Los Angeles, but FIFA did not want Olympic football to be as big as the World Cup. Now only three players in each men's Olympic football team can be over twenty-three years old. But the women's teams, who have played Olympic football since 1996, can have players of any age.

Mia Hamm (USA) and Elaine (Brazil) in the Olympic Final, 2004

6   Women's football

Women have always played football – from games of *Tsu Chu* in China more than 2,000 years ago, to women's matches in Scotland in 1892 and in England in 1895. But it was at the beginning of the twentieth century that women really began to get interested in football.

During the First World War (1914–1918) many women began to work in factories. At lunchtime they often played football, and the first women's teams were factory teams. The most famous team was from the Dick, Kerr factory in Preston in the north of England, and their star player was Lily Parr. Lily joined the Dick, Kerr's Ladies team in 1919 at the age of fourteen. She was nearly 180 cm tall and was a wonderful striker, scoring forty-three goals in her first season.

Dick, Kerr International Ladies, 1921

Women were starting to play football in France too, and in 1920 there were matches between England and France, with a crowd of 25,000 at the first game. But not everybody was happy about women's matches. In December 1921 the Football Association in England told clubs that they must not let women play on their grounds, and the Scottish Football Association soon did the same.

What was wrong with women playing football? 'They'll get hurt', 'They show too much leg', and worst of all, 'It's just not very nice' were the answers. Perhaps another reason was that the women's matches took people (and money) away from the men's games. But women went on playing on rugby grounds and other places.

At last, in 1971, the English Football Association said that women could play on club grounds. And in the 1970s and 1980s women in many countries began to enjoy playing football. (In 1970 the German Football Association said that women could now play football – but only in the warm months!) Then in 1991 teams from twelve countries went to China for the first FIFA Women's World Cup. A crowd of 63,000 saw the USA beat Norway 2–1 in the final. In 2007, there were sixteen countries in the cup, and the winners were the team from Germany.

Life is much harder for women footballers than for men. Many women get little or no money for playing, so they have to have a job at the same time. Fewer people come to see their matches, and women's matches do not get as much time on TV. A lot of men (and some women too) speak badly of women who play. So the women who become football stars have to work very hard to get to the top.

Birgit Prinz winning the Women's World Cup with Germany, 2007

Mia Hamm played for seventeen years for the USA national team and was twice FIFA World Player of the Year. Pelé included her in his list of 125 greatest living footballers. She is the youngest woman to play in a team that won the World Cup (aged nineteen, playing for the USA in 1991). She scored 158 goals in international matches – more than anyone else, man or woman.

Sun Wen played for China from 1990 to 2006. She played in the World Cup team three times, and with Michelle Akers of the USA she was named FIFA's Woman Player of the Century in 2000.

Birgit Prinz has been Germany's Women's Footballer of the Year many times, and was FIFA's Woman Player of the Year in 2003, 2004, and 2005. She played in the German team for four World Cups, winning twice. In 2003 AC Perugia, a top Italian team, asked her to play in their *men's* team – but she said no.

The Brazilian player Marta followed Birgit Prinz as FIFA's Woman Player of the Year in 2006 (when she was aged only twenty) and in 2007. Many people say that she is the best woman player in the world and the great player Pelé has called her 'Pelé in skirts'. At the 2007 World Cup she won the Golden Ball (best player) and the Golden Shoe (best scorer). Marta is fast and clever and a great goal scorer.

What is in the future for women's football? More than 26 million women play football around the world, and the numbers are getting bigger all the time. In 2009 the USA will try for a second time to have a professional league for women, called Women's Professional Soccer. Women footballers everywhere hope that this new league will do well.

Marta playing for Brazil

7   Stars of football

There are good players and great players – and then there are the stars. These five players are all in FIFA's list of 100 greatest living footballers.

Pelé Many people think that Edison Arantes do Nascimento from Brazil – better known as Pelé or King Pelé or the King of Football – is the greatest football player of all time.

Pelé was born in 1940 into a poor family. At the age of seventeen, he played in his first World Cup in 1958 – the youngest player ever to play in a World Cup. He played in three more Brazilian World Cup teams, in 1962, 1966, and 1970. (Three of these teams – in 1958, 1962, and 1970 – went on to win the cup.) In the 1970 World Cup

Pelé, after the 1970 World Cup Final

final he scored the first goal for Brazil and helped to make two more. Pelé was named Footballer of the Century by FIFA in 2000.

Pelé was a striker: he was fast and strong and clever. He could run round players with the ball and he could head the ball. He was beautiful to watch. But most of all, he could score goals. He scored 1,281 goals for clubs and country! Today Pelé works for football, for his country, and for UNICEF, which tries to make a better life for children everywhere.

Brazilians say that their country is 'the football country', and they have won the World Cup five times, more than any other country. After the third time, in 1970, they kept the cup – but someone stole it in 1983.

Diego Maradona Argentina is also a big name

in South American football, and the greatest and most famous Argentinian footballer of the 1980s was Diego Maradona. Some people say that he was as good as Pelé.

Like Pelé, Maradona was born into a poor family. He was short and strong, and could travel very fast with the ball. He played for Argentina in four World Cups, and was captain when Argentina won in 1986. One of his goals in the 1986 World Cup quarter-finals was called 'Goal of the Century'. He also played for great European clubs like Barcelona and Napoli. Maradona did not play for Argentina after 1994, but he was a great footballer and he helped to make Argentina a very good team in the 1980s. He was named Internet Player of the Century by FIFA in 2000.

Maradona in the 1986 World Cup

Argentina has won the World Cup twice – in 1978 and 1986 – and has won the Copa América many times. Games between Argentina and Brazil are usually very exciting, and the fans from both countries sing and make a noise from the beginning of the match to the end.

Zinedine Zidane

The French-Algerian player Zinedine Zidane played for France for twelve years, and was in the team that won the World Cup for France in 1998. He played for teams in France, and then for top teams Juventus in Italy and Real Madrid in Spain.

Zidane sometimes got angry during games, and many times referees showed him the red card. The most famous time was near the end of the World Cup final in 2006, after Zidane hit the Italian player Marco Materazzi with his head. But Zidane was a very clever and popular player. Only two players have been FIFA World Player of the Year three times; Zidane is one, and the Brazilian player Ronaldo is the other.

The World Cup win in 1998 was a great moment for France, but there have been many other great French players in world football, for example Michel Platini, Eric Cantona, Thierry Henry, and Patrick Vieira.

Zinedine Zidane

David Beckham

Beckham was captain of the English team for fifty-eight games over six years. He is one of only five players who have played for England more than 100 times.

For ten years Beckham played for the rich and popular club Manchester United. During that time the club won the English Premier League six times and the FA Cup twice. He then went to play for the Spanish club Real Madrid, and left them in 2007 for Los Angeles Galaxy.

Beckham is one of the best-known and highest-paid footballers in the world. Newspapers are always full of news about his hair, his clothes, his wife Victoria, and his family. But Beckham has given a lot back to the game. At the two David Beckham Academies, in London and Los Angeles, young footballers can learn to play better football.

Like France, England has won the World Cup once, in 1966. To many people, England is the home of football. It has more clubs than any other country, and its top clubs, like Arsenal, Chelsea, Liverpool, and Manchester United, are popular with fans all over the world.

David Beckham taking a free kick

Nakata playing for Japan

Hidetoshi Nakata

Nakata played from 1995 to 2006, and in that short time he played for Japan in three World Cups. He was Asian Player of the Year in 1997 and 1998, before leaving Japan for Italy. There he played for five top clubs; among them were AS Roma, Perugia, and Parma. He stopped playing professional football after the World Cup in 2006, but he did not stop playing football. Now he travels the world, making friends, playing matches, and helping to bring football to people who want to play.

It is not surprising that Nakata went to play in Italy, the top country for football in Europe. Italy has won the World Cup four times – only one less than Brazil – and clubs like Juventus and AC Milan are among the strongest in Europe.

So this is one list of great footballers, but everybody has their own favourite stars – players, clubs, or countries. Who is on *your* list?

8 The business of football

When the great English football player Sir Stanley Matthews played for Blackpool and England in the 1950s, he got about 40 dollars a week. Today some of the top players in Europe get more than 85 thousand dollars a week. Football today is big money and big business.

Players get all this money because the top clubs want to win and stay on top. And a lot of the money comes from the pockets of their supporters. The cheapest tickets to see teams like Barcelona, Juventus, and Manchester United cost 40 dollars or more. Football was once a game for ordinary people, but tickets at these prices are too expensive for many of them. Money is much more important in football than before.

Some rich clubs are getting richer, but many other clubs are getting poorer. In England again, a place in the Premier League gives each club more than 55 million dollars from TV companies. Few teams in other divisions get more than 1.5 million dollars. Once most football matches were played at 3 o'clock on Saturday afternoons, after men finished work in the factories. Now the TV companies tell the clubs to play their matches at different times on Saturdays and Sundays and through the week. That way people watching at home can see more matches

Stanley Matthews (left) in the 1950s

– and the TV companies can make more money. The fans and the clubs do not decide these things any more.

Fifty years ago, most clubs belonged to local businessmen, but that is changing. Russian billionaire Roman Abramovich bought Chelsea Football Club in the English Premier League in 2003, and in 2008 nine of the twenty top clubs in England belonged to foreign owners. This is beginning to happen in other European countries too: there are Italian and French clubs with American owners, for example. Is this a bad thing? A rich owner can bring a lot of money to a club, but some supporters worry that foreign owners are more interested in the business than the football.

Now there are foreign fans too. In the past, most of a club's fans lived in or near the town or city that gave its name to the club. Today top teams can have fans all over the world. Between 100 and 340 million people in China watch English Premier League matches on television. Both Barcelona and Real Madrid have travelled to Asia and have thousands of fans there.

At the same time, top European clubs have many foreign players, from Africa, Asia, and the Americas. In 2005 Frenchman Arsène Wenger, the manager of Arsenal, named sixteen men to play for the club in a match: for the first time in the Premier League, not one of them was English. People say that England does not have a good national team because there are so many foreign players playing in English teams.

African players now leave their own countries to play for richer European clubs. This means that people in their own countries cannot see them playing any more.

So, is all this money good or bad for the game? More men, women, and children are watching and playing football than ever before. The game is bringing people from different countries together as players and fans. Yet some clubs are more like businesses than sports clubs now. The fans are paying more and more money for tickets, and the players are getting richer and richer. Where will it stop?

Manchester United in Macao, 2007

9 The dark side of football

On 22 June 1994, Andrés Escobar of Colombia scored a goal in a World Cup match against the United States. But he put the ball into the wrong goal: he scored for the USA. The USA won the match and the Colombian team went home early. On 2 July, Escobar was leaving a restaurant in Medellín with his girlfriend when two men came up to them. They were angry about the goal, and one of the men had a gun. A few minutes later, Escobar was dead.

Football has always had a dark side. People feel very strongly about the game, sometimes too strongly. When teams win, their fans are happy but sometimes when a team loses, its fans get angry and then there are problems. And then there are billions of dollars in the game, and some of that money comes from crime. Football can be exciting, but it can be dangerous too.

Crowds One big problem in football is crowds. When large numbers of excited people come together at big matches, sometimes the crowd begins to push. Then people fall to the ground and die. In 1964, 301 people died at a match between Argentina and Peru in Lima. Sixty-six people died at Ibrox Stadium, the home of Glasgow Rangers in Scotland, when crowds of people began pushing

down the stairs after a match in 1971. In 1982, 340 people died at a match between Spartak Moscow and Haarlem of Holland. Ninety-five people died at a match between Liverpool and Nottingham Forest at the Hillsborough stadium in Sheffield, England in 1989. These terrible deaths often happened when people were standing, not sitting, to watch the games, so now many clubs have changed their stadiums and put in seats for everyone.

Hooligans

Hooligans go to football matches to make trouble. They try to fight the supporters of the other team inside and outside the stadium. The problem of hooligans is not new: an angry crowd stopped the players leaving the pitch at a game in England in 1885. But hooligans were a very big problem in England in the 1980s and 1990s. Hooligans went to matches by train and broke everything in the trains. Then they fought and broke shop windows in the streets after the matches. Many people were afraid to go into the street on the day of a football match. And England was not the only country with these problems. Countries like Italy, Russia, Turkey, Germany, and Argentina also had trouble, with fights and sometimes deaths at football matches.

Today things are better. Games now are not so dangerous, because the police understand the problem better and because the stadiums have seats for all the supporters. The police know how to work with large numbers of people. They also take photos of the dangerous fans and use cameras to find them. Then they stop these people from going to football matches and from going to other countries with their teams.

Cheating There are always people who cheat in sport, and it happens in football too. In 2006 the Italian police found that famous Serie A teams like Juventus, AC Milan, Lazio, Fiorentina, and Reggina were having secret talks with referees before matches, and deciding who would win. In Germany in 2005, the referee Robert Hoyzer told police that he took money from clubs before matches. In England, the Arsenal manager George Graham lost his job in 1995 when he took money during the buying and selling of players. All this is very bad for the good name of football not just in Italy, Germany, and England, but across the world.

Hooligans and police

10 Football today and tomorrow

Football has changed a lot in the last hundred years – the players' clothes are different, their shoes are not so heavy, and there are new rules. How will things change in the next twenty-five years?

An international game

Fifty years ago, most football was played in Europe and South America and most of the important teams came from these countries. Today football is everywhere in the world. There has been a World Cup in the USA. Europeans watch the Africa Cup of Nations on TV. Perhaps in the next twenty-five years, African and Asian teams will be better than the Europeans and South Americans.

Football in the USA

In the USA, people have always played and watched American football much more than soccer. Businessmen and players often tried to make soccer a big TV sport but it never worked. People said: 'Soccer is the sport of tomorrow in the US – and always will be.' Millions of Americans watched soccer for the first time in 1994, when the World Cup matches were played in the USA, and the American team was in the last sixteen. Now more than 3 million young people in America play soccer. Perhaps in the future the number of older players and fans will get bigger too.

New rules for football Could football be more exciting with different rules? Big business, TV, and some fans think so. They want to make the goals bigger; or stop the offside rule; or have a referee with a TV who can help the referee on the pitch; or give the referee another card (blue or green perhaps) to send players off for 10 or 15 minutes only. With some of these changes the game could be faster, more interesting, and have more goals. Perhaps the score in the 2018 World Cup final will be 11–9 . . .

Technology Computers have come to football. They can tell managers how far a player runs and where he runs, how many times he touches the ball, how many good and bad passes he makes, how many times he shoots, and many more things. This information helps managers to understand their own team and other teams. Perhaps it can help the players to play better football too.

Superleagues The big clubs in Europe talk about making a European superleague. If this happens,

the best European teams will stop playing in their national leagues and will play each other. They could get a lot of money from these games. But if there is a superleague, it will be bad for smaller clubs. The big money will go to the big clubs, and the money problems of the small clubs will get worse.

We'll support you evermore

The fans sing, 'We'll support you evermore,' but nobody knows how football will change. Football is always full of surprises. New players, teams, and champions are out there, waiting for their moment.

Perhaps in the future people will look back at the World Cup in South Africa in 2010 and say, 'That was the beginning of African teams in world football'. Perhaps in 2018 an Asian team will be the world champion. Nobody knows, but one thing is sure – more people than ever will enjoy the beautiful game.

GLOSSARY

beat to win a game against a group of people

blow to send air out from your mouth

card a piece of thick paper

champion the person or team that is the best at a sport;
championship *(n)* a competition to find the champion

club a sports organization with players, managers, and
supporters, etc.

competition a number of games that people or teams try to win

control to have power over something

corner (in football) a free kick from the corner near the other
team's goal

crazy mad; very excited about something

defend to try to stop another team from scoring goals

fan a person who likes something very much

final the last game in a competition

flag a piece of coloured cloth on a stick

foreign from a country that is not your own

game something that you play that has rules, e.g. football, tennis,
rugby, etc.

goal a point that a football team gets when they put the ball into
the net; the place at the end of the field where goals are made

head *(v)* to hit a football with your head

international connected with two or more countries

kick to hit something with your foot

kind a group of things that are the same in some way

last *(v)* to continue for a certain amount of time

league a group of teams that play each other to find which team
is the best

local belonging to a particular place

manage to control a team or a business; **manager** *(n)*

match a game between two teams

national belonging to a particular country

organization a group of people who work together for a special purpose

part one of the pieces of something

pass (*n & v*) to kick or hit the ball to another player on your team

penalty a chance for your team to score a goal when the other team has broken the rules

point a number that you add to your total when you score a goal or win a game

referee the person who controls a football game

region a part of a country or of the world; **regional** (*adj*)

rule something that tells you what you must or must not do in a game

score (*n & v*) to get a goal

shoot to try to kick the ball into the goal

support to like a particular team and go to their games, etc.; **supporter** (*n*)

team a group of people who play together against another group

throw to use your hand(*s*) to send something quickly through the air

university a place where people go to study after they leave school

whistle a small metal tube that makes a long high sound when you blow it

Football: The Beautiful Game

ACTIVITIES

ACTIVITIES

―――――――

Before Reading

1 **Read the back cover of the book, and the introduction on the first page. You will find these words. Can you match them with the definitions?**

cup, fan, final, goal, kick, league, rules, star, team

1 _____ The last, most important game in a competition

2 _____ A group of eleven football players who play together

3 _____ A person who loves a sport, and often watches it on TV or goes to matches

4 _____ These tell players what they must and must not do

5 _____ The winners of a competition get this

6 _____ Someone who is very famous, for example a movie actor or sports player

7 _____ To hit a ball with your foot

8 _____ When the ball goes past the goalkeeper and into the net

9 _____ A group of teams that play each other to find which team is the best

2 **Do you know any other words about football? What are they, and what do they mean?**

3 **How much do you know about the rules of football? Write some sentences with *must*, *mustn't*, and *can*. For example:**

The goalkeeper can touch the ball with his hands.

ACTIVITIES

While Reading

Read Chapters 1 and 2. Are these sentences true (T) or false (F)?

1 The first FIFA World Cup competition was in Uruguay.

2 Millions watched the first World Cup Final on TV.

3 Three of the European teams in the first World Cup travelled across the Atlantic in the same aeroplane.

4 There are more than 1.5 million football teams in the world.

5 Rugby was first played in England.

6 The referee adds 'injury time' at the end of the game if both teams have the same number of goals.

7 Subbuteo is a football game that you can play on a table.

Read Chapter 3, then fill in the gaps with these words.

flag, foul, goalkeeper, striker, throw-in, whistle

1 The match starts when the referee blows the _____.

2 If the ball goes outside the lines on the pitch, there is a _____.

3 If a player is offside, the assistant referee holds up their _____.

4 It is a _____ if a player kicks another player.

5 The _____ is the only player who can touch the ball with their hands.

6 The job of a _____ is to attack and score goals.

Read Chapters 4 and 5. Match these halves of sentences.

1 In Ashbourne, they play a game of football that . . .
2 In the past, many English kings . . .
3 In 1863 a group of men met in London to . . .
4 The first international match in the world was . . .
5 In England the football season . . .
6 Teams get three points . . .
7 The FIFA World Cup happens . . .
8 In a men's Olympic football team, only three players . . .

a every four years.
b between England and Scotland.
c tried to stop football because they did not like it.
d start the Football Association.
e lasts from August to May.
f can be over twenty-three years old.
g takes two days.
h when they win a game.

Read Chapter 6, then complete the sentences with these names.

Mia Hamm / Marta / Lily Parr / Birgit Prinz / Sun Wen

1 . . . was fourteen when she joined her factory's football team.
2 . . . scored more goals in international matches than any other player.
3 . . . was named FIFA's Woman Player of the Century in the year 2000.
4 . . . was asked to play in a top Italian men's team.
5 . . . was a top player at the 2007 World Cup.

Read Chapter 7. Choose the best question-words for these questions, and then answer them.

How long / How many / How old / Where / Who / Why

1 . . . was Pelé when he played in his first World Cup?
2 . . . times has Brazil won the World Cup?
3 . . . helped to make Argentina a very good team?
4 . . . did the referee show Zidane the red card in the 2006 World Cup Final?
5 . . . did David Beckham play for Manchester United?
6 . . . did Hidetoshi Nakata go when he left Japan?

Read Chapter 8, then circle the correct words.

1 These days the big clubs use a lot of the money from tickets to pay for *time on television / star players*.
2 Clubs in the English Premier League get a lot of money from *newspaper / television* companies.
3 In the past, most football matches in England were played on *Saturday afternoons / Friday evenings*.
4 In 2003, a *Russian / Japanese* billionaire bought Chelsea Football Club.
5 In 2005, a team that played for the English club Arsenal was unusual because *all / none* of its players were English.

Before you read Chapter 9 (*The dark side of football*), can you guess what it is about? Write Y (yes) or N (no) next to each subject.

1 Fighting between players
2 Terrible accidents that happen at football matches
3 Players who leave their club to play in another country
4 Fighting between fans

Read Chapter 9, then circle a, b, c, or d.

1 In the 1994 World Cup between Colombia and the USA,
   Andrés Escobar _____.
   a) didn't score   c) scored for Colombia
   b) scored for the USA   d) didn't play

2 _____ are people who go to football matches to make
   trouble.
   a) Supporters   c) Hooligans
   b) Strikers   d) Defenders

3 Games are not so dangerous now, because there are _____
   for all the supporters at most stadiums.
   a) seats c) whistles
   b) numbers   d) flags

4 In 2005, a German referee told police that some _____ gave
   him money before matches.
   a) players   c) supporters
   b) assistant referees   d) clubs

Read Chapter 10. Complete the summary with these words.

*Africa, best, changed, first, less, most, only, prefer, small,
watched*

Football has _____ a lot in the last hundred years. Now,
football is not played _____ in Europe and South America
– there are clubs in _____ and Asia too. Millions of
Americans _____ soccer for the _____ time in 1994, but
_____ people in the USA still _____ American football.
Perhaps there will be a 'superleague' for the _____
European teams. If this happens, there will be more money
for the big clubs but _____ money for the _____ clubs.

ACTIVITIES

After Reading

1 **Match the people with the sentences. Then use the sentences to write a short description of each person. Use pronouns (*he, she*) and linking words (*and, but, so, who*).**

Zinedine Zidane / Pelé / King Richard the Second of England / Birgit Prinz / Robert Hoyzer / Diego Maradona

1 _____ was FIFA Woman Player of the Year three times.

2 _____ was a German referee.

3 _____ was a short, strong player.

4 _____ played for France for twelve years.

5 _____ was born into a poor family in Brazil.

6 _____ did not like football.

7 _____ was in the team that won the 1998 World Cup.

8 _____ played in a World Cup when he was seventeen.

9 _____ played for Germany in four World Cups.

10 _____ sometimes took money from clubs before matches.

11 _____ scored the 'Goal of the Century' in 1986.

12 _____ said that all football must stop.

13 _____ works for UNICEF now, helping children.

14 _____ got into trouble and had to talk to the police.

15 _____ sometimes got angry, and had to leave the field.

16 _____ decided not to play for an Italian men's team.

17 _____ was captain of Argentina when they won the World Cup in 1986.

18 _____ was not able to stop people from playing football.

**2 Use the clues below to complete this crossword with words
from *The Beautiful Game*. Then find the hidden word.**

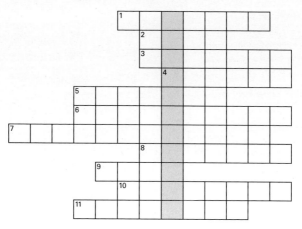

1 The first women football players worked at a ____.

2 The World Cup is played every ____ years.

3 An ____ player does not get any money for playing football.

4 In a football league competition, teams get three ____ when
   they win a game.

5 The ____ were playing a ball game 2,000 years ago.

6 If a player is tired or hurt, a ____ can take their place.

7 A ____ player gets money for playing football.

8 Important matches are played in a big ____.

9 The two winners of the ____-finals play in the final.

10 Gaelic, American, and Australian Rules are all kinds of

   ____.

11 A ____ must stay close to the other team's strikers.

What's the hidden word? Can you find examples in the book?

3 **There is one word in each group that does not belong. Which is it? Then choose the best heading for each group from the list below.**

equipment, famous players, kinds of player, moving the ball

1 _____: ball, flag, net, point, whistle
2 _____: head, kick, pass, rule, throw
3 _____: Abramovich, Beckham, Hamm, Nakata, Zidane
4 _____: defender, goalkeeper, manager, midfielder, striker

4 **Do you agree or disagree with these sentences? Say why.**

	AGREE	DISAGREE
Football players get too much money.	☐	☐
There is often trouble at football matches.	☐	☐
Tickets to football matches are too expensive.	☐	☐
There is too much football on television.	☐	☐
Referees give penalties too easily.	☐	☐
Having many foreign players in a team is bad.	☐	☐
It's bad for players to get angry.	☐	☐

5 **Make a poster about a football club in your country. Look for answers to these questions:**

When did the club start?

Which league does the team play in?

Has the club ever won any competitions?

Where is the stadium?

Who are the best players in the club? Are they strikers, defenders, or midfield players?

ABOUT THE AUTHOR

Steve Flinders has lived and worked in Pakistan, Sweden, Ireland, and France as well as in the UK. He now lives in the beautiful city of York in the north of England and is a director of a training company, York Associates. His wife is French-Italian and they have three sons, one of whom is a keen footballer.

Steve teaches business people and politicians in York and all over Europe but spends most Saturday afternoons from August to May watching his son playing football. When he can, he also watches Derby County, the team he has supported ever since they were the best team in England, more than thirty years ago. He dreams that one day they will be the best team again although he knows that this may take some time. In his spare time he likes reading, talking politics, going to the theatre, swimming, playing squash badly, and sleeping. He is a terrible footballer.

OXFORD BOOKWORMS LIBRARY

Classics • Crime & Mystery • Factfiles • Fantasy & Horror
Human Interest • Playscripts • Thriller & Adventure
True Stories • World Stories

The OXFORD BOOKWORMS LIBRARY provides enjoyable reading in English, with a wide range of classic and modern fiction, non-fiction, and plays. It includes original and adapted texts in seven carefully graded language stages, which take learners from beginner to advanced level. An overview is given on the next pages.

All Stage 1 titles are available as audio recordings, as well as over eighty other titles from Starter to Stage 6. All Starters and many titles at Stages 1 to 4 are specially recommended for younger learners. Every Bookworm is illustrated, and Starters and Factfiles have full-colour illustrations.

The OXFORD BOOKWORMS LIBRARY also offers extensive support. Each book contains an introduction to the story, notes about the author, a glossary, and activities. Additional resources include tests and worksheets, and answers for these and for the activities in the books. There is advice on running a class library, using audio recordings, and the many ways of using Oxford Bookworms in reading programmes. Resource materials are available on the website <www.oup.com/elt/gradedreaders>.

The *Oxford Bookworms Collection* is a series for advanced learners. It consists of volumes of short stories by well-known authors, both classic and modern. Texts are not abridged or adapted in any way, but carefully selected to be accessible to the advanced student.

You can find details and a full list of titles in the *Oxford Bookworms Library Catalogue* and *Oxford English Language Teaching Catalogues,* and on the website <www.oup.com/elt/gradedreaders>.

THE OXFORD BOOKWORMS LIBRARY
GRADING AND SAMPLE EXTRACTS

STARTER • 250 HEADWORDS

present simple – present continuous – imperative –
can/cannot, must – *going to* (future) – simple gerunds …

Her phone is ringing – but where is it?

Sally gets out of bed and looks in her bag. No phone. She looks under the bed. No phone. Then she looks behind the door. There is her phone. Sally picks up her phone and answers it. *Sally's Phone*

STAGE 1 • 400 HEADWORDS

… past simple – coordination with *and*, *but*, *or* –
subordination with *before, after, when, because, so* …

I knew him in Persia. He was a famous builder and I worked with him there. For a time I was his friend, but not for long. When he came to Paris, I came after him – I wanted to watch him. He was a very clever, very dangerous man. *The Phantom of the Opera*

STAGE 2 • 700 HEADWORDS

… present perfect – *will* (future) – *(don't) have to, must not, could* –
comparison of adjectives – simple *if* clauses – past continuous –
tag questions – *ask/tell* + infinitive …

While I was writing these words in my diary, I decided what to do. I must try to escape. I shall try to get down the wall outside. The window is high above the ground, but I have to try. I shall take some of the gold with me – if I escape, perhaps it will be helpful later. *Dracula*

STAGE 3 • 1000 HEADWORDS

... should, may – present perfect continuous – *used to* – past perfect
– causative – relative clauses – indirect statements ...

Of course, it was most important that no one should see
Colin, Mary, or Dickon entering the secret garden. So Colin
gave orders to the gardeners that they must all keep away
from that part of the garden in future. *The Secret Garden*

STAGE 4 • 1400 HEADWORDS

*... past perfect continuous – passive (simple forms) –
would* conditional clauses – indirect questions –
relatives with *where/when* – gerunds after prepositions/phrases ...

I was glad. Now Hyde could not show his face to the world
again. If he did, every honest man in London would be
proud to report him to the police. *Dr Jekyll and Mr Hyde*

STAGE 5 • 1800 HEADWORDS

... future continuous – future perfect –
passive (modals, continuous forms) –
would have conditional clauses – modals + perfect infinitive ...

If he had spoken Estella's name, I would have hit him. I was
so angry with him, and so depressed about my future, that I
could not eat the breakfast. Instead I went straight to the old
house. *Great Expectations*

STAGE 6 • 2500 HEADWORDS

... passive (infinitives, gerunds) – advanced modal meanings –
clauses of concession, condition

When I stepped up to the piano, I was confident. It was as if I
knew that the prodigy side of me really did exist. And when I
started to play, I was so caught up in how lovely I looked that
I didn't worry how I would sound. *The Joy Luck Club*

BOOKWORMS · FACTFILES · STAGE 2

Seasons and Celebrations

JACKIE MAGUIRE

In English-speaking countries around the world people celebrate Easter, Valentine's Day, Christmas, and other special days. Some celebrations are new, like Remembrance Day and Mother's Day; others, like the summer solstice, go back thousands of years.

What happens on these special days? What do people eat, where do they go, what do they do? Why is there a special day for eating pancakes? Who is the 'guy' that children take onto the streets in November? And where do many people like to spend the shortest night of the year in England? Come on a journey through a year of celebrations, from New Year's Eve to Christmas.

BOOKWORMS · FACTFILES · STAGE 2

Ireland

TIM VICARY

There are many different Irelands. There is the Ireland of peaceful rivers, green fields, and beautiful islands. There is the Ireland of song and dance, pubs and theatres – the country of James Joyce, Bob Geldof, and Riverdance. And there is the Ireland of guns, fighting, death, and the hope of peace. Come with us and visit all of these Irelands – and many more . . .